Seeing

Lillian Wright

Watts Books
London • New York • Sydney

© 1994 Watts Books

Watts Books
96 Leonard Street
London EC2A 4RH

Franklin Watts Australia
14 Mars Road
Lane Cove
NSW 2060

UK ISBN: 0 7496 1204 5

Design: Sally Boothroyd
Artwork: Mainline Design
Cover artwork: Jonathan Gill

A CIP catalogue record for this book
is available from the British Library

Dewey Decimal Classification 612.84

Printed in Italy by G. Canale & SpA

Contents

Introduction

We use our eyes to see. We are able to see many things in the world around us if our eyes are working properly. We can see very small things that are close to us and very large things that are far away. We can also see many different colours.

▽ Seeing is one of our five senses.

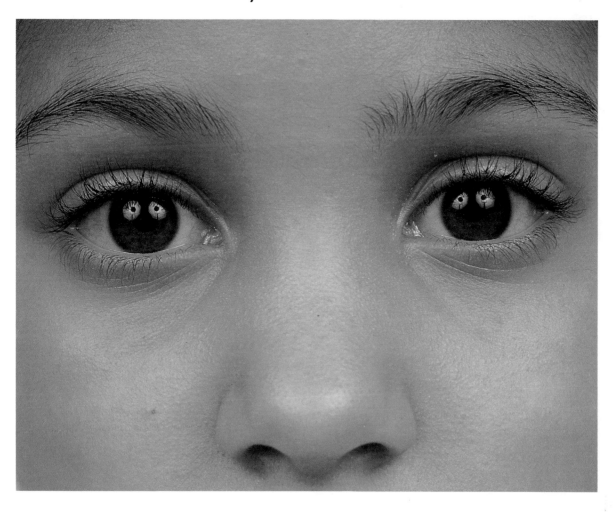

3

Looking closely

Our eyes are like little balls, protected by our bony skull. When we look in a mirror we can only see the front part of our eyes. This part is kept clean by our eyelids and tears from our tear ducts. Together, they wash our eyes each time we blink. Our eyebrows and eyelashes stop dirt and sweat getting into our eyes.

▽ Salty tears wash away any dirt that gets in our eyes.

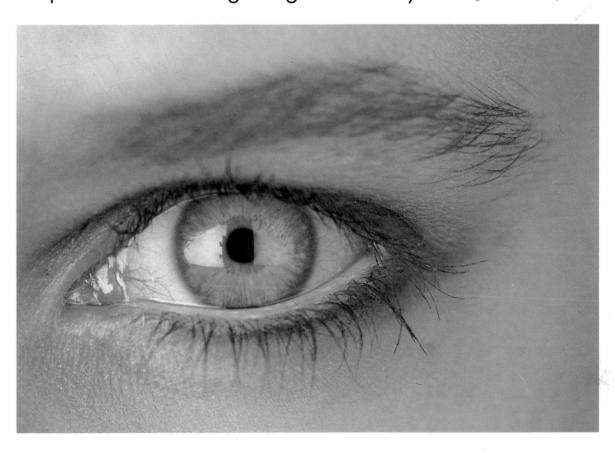

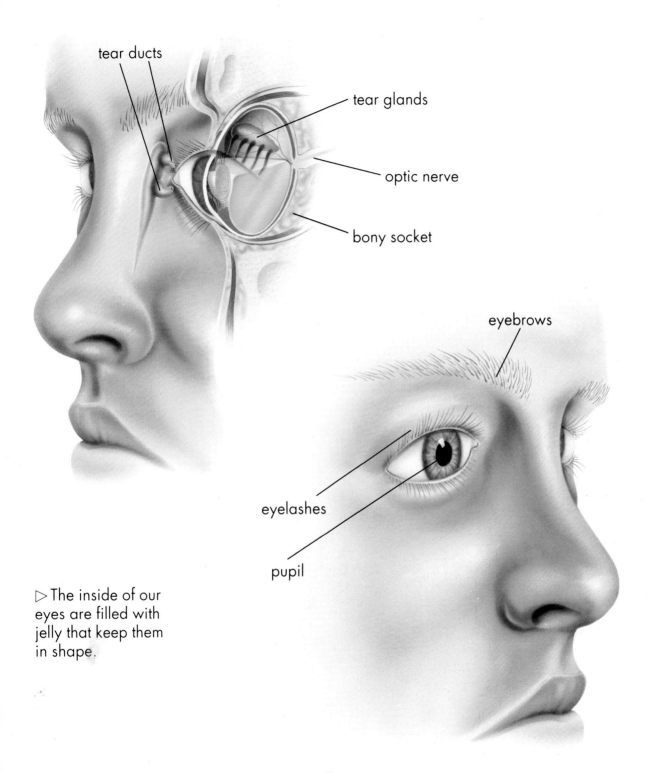

tear ducts

tear glands

optic nerve

bony socket

eyebrows

eyelashes

pupil

▷ The inside of our eyes are filled with jelly that keep them in shape.

Eyes are different

We all have two eyes, but they can look very different. Some people have brown eyes, other people may have blue or green eyes. Sometimes a person may have two eyes of different colours. In some parts of the world the common eye shape may be oval. In other parts of the world the eyes may be much narrower.

▷ Animals also have different eye shapes. An owl has two large, round eyes which help it to hunt small creatures.

△ Our eyes come in
all shapes, sizes and
colours.

7

Eyes and light

Our eyes need light to see. Lights goes into our eyes through the **pupil**. This is the little black circle which we can see in the middle of our eyes. The coloured part of our eye, called the **iris**, can make the pupil bigger or smaller. This stops our eyes being hurt by too much light.

▽ Very bright light can damage our eyes. NEVER look directly at the sun. Sunglasses help protect our eyes in bright light.

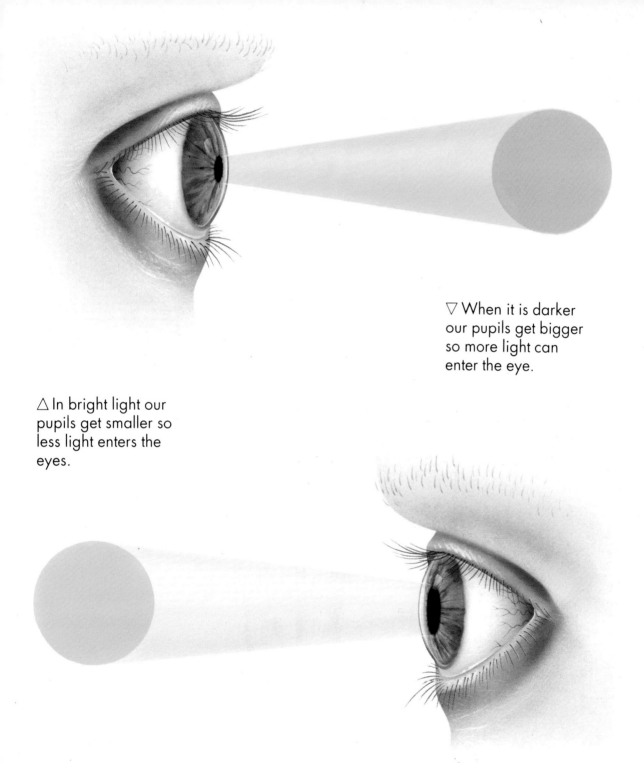

▽ When it is darker
our pupils get bigger
so more light can
enter the eye.

△ In bright light our
pupils get smaller so
less light enters the
eyes.

How do we see?

Your eye works like a camera. Light enters and passes through the **lens**. It forms an upside-down image on the sensitive part at the back of the eye called the **retina**. Inside the retina are nerve cells, called rods and cones, which send constant messages to the brain through the **optic nerve** about what we are seeing. The brain sorts out the image and turns it the right way round.

▽ The retina is sensitive to even very small amounts of light.

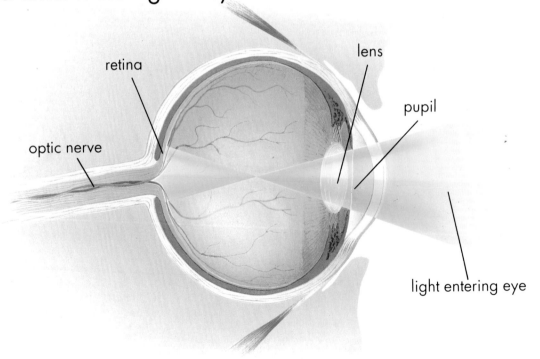

retina

lens

pupil

optic nerve

light entering eye

▷If this miner switches off his lamp, he will not be able to see anything.

▽ Wearing a blindfold prevents light entering our eyes and stops us being able to see. But even if we cannot see where a sound is coming from, our ears will be able to tell us.

Eye care

We need to take care of our eyes. They are not easy to repair if we hurt them, so we should always be very careful. People who work with machines or tools wear special glasses or visors to protect their eyes. In school, children may wear goggles in science lessons to stop their eyes being damaged accidentally.

▷ If we damage our eyes we can go blind. Sometimes operations can be performed to save damaged eyes.

▽ Some jobs, such as welding, would be dangerous if people did not protect their eyes.

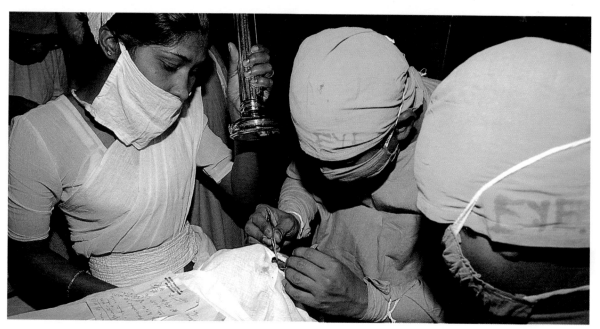

▽ Dust and dirt in
towns and cities may
irritate and scratch
the delicate surface
of our eyes.

How well can you see?

We all have two eyes but we cannot all see equally well. Sometimes people cannot focus properly. This usually happens because either the lens or the whole eye is the wrong shape. People are **short-sighted** if they cannot see things far away, and **long-sighted** if they cannot see things close to them.

▷ Older people may find it hard to read small print because the muscles that change the shape of the lens in their eyes grow slack with age.

▽ The eye focuses by changing the shape of the lens.

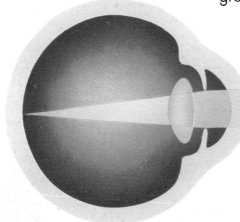

▽ To focus on distant objects, the lens grows flatter.

△ To focus on close objects, the lens bulges outwards.

Why do we wear glasses?

The lenses in our eyes help us to see clearly by focussing the images we see. If our lenses are not working properly we may have to wear glasses. These have their own lenses which help the person see better. In older people the lens may get very cloudy. A doctor can carefully take this out and the person wears glasses instead.

▷ The lenses of glasses are kept in place by frames of all shapes and colours.

▽ People called opticians test our eyesight to see if we need to wear glasses.

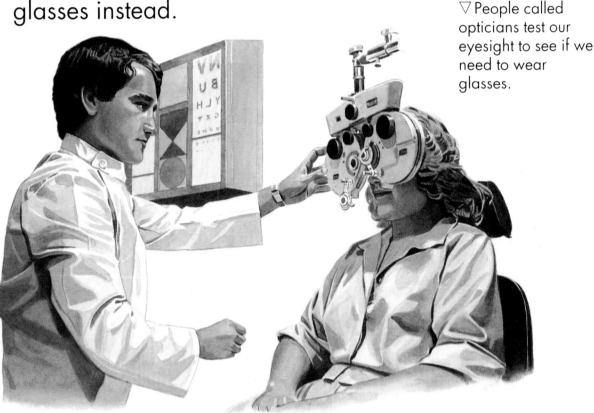

▽ Some people wear contact lenses instead of glasses.

Partial sight and blindness

A baby may be born blind. Sometimes an accident or illness may make a person blind. Some people may not be completely blind, but can only see things that are very close to them. This is called partial sight. Life is more difficult for these people. They cannot read books or watch television, but they can listen to taped stories and 'read' **Braille** with their fingertips.

▷ The letters in Braille books are made up of a series of raised dots which are felt with the fingertips.

△ Some blind or partially-sighted people have a specially-trained dog to guide them.

▷ This blind person listens and feels his way along the street using a stick to let him know what is in front of him.

Seeing colour

Our eyes are able to see a very large number of different colours. We see colours best in bright light. At night when there is less light entering our eyes we see the shape and size of things clearly but not their colour. Some people are not able to see all colours. This is called **colour blindness**.

▽ When there is less light, such as at dusk, we do not see colours as well.

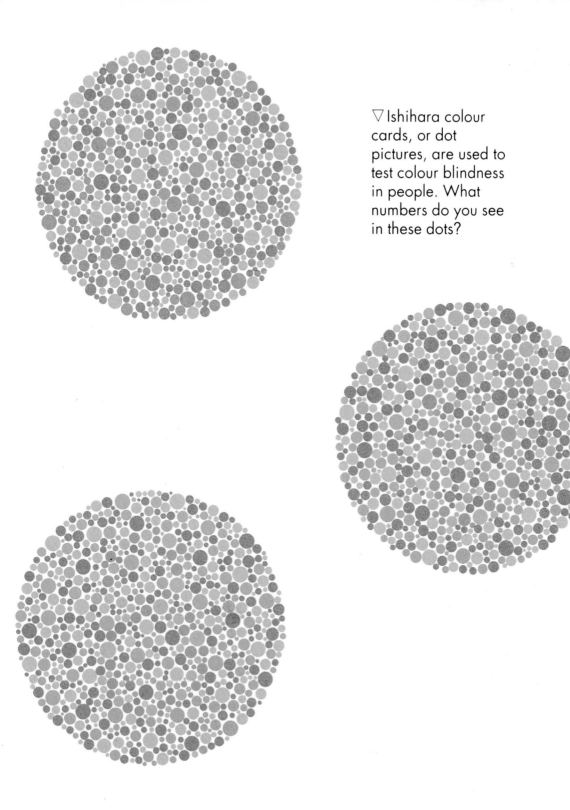

▽ Ishihara colour cards, or dot pictures, are used to test colour blindness in people. What numbers do you see in these dots?

Why have two eyes?

If we only had one eye we could still see things around us, but we would not be able to judge distances very well. Our two eyes do not see exactly the same picture of the world. Our brain overlaps the two pictures our two eyes give us. This is called **stereoscopic vision**. It also makes objects seem solid, or three-dimensional, rather than flat.

▷ With one eye covered it is difficult to tell how far away something is.

▽ Flies have two huge compound eyes, with thousands of six-sided lenses. But in spite of this, they cannot see very well.

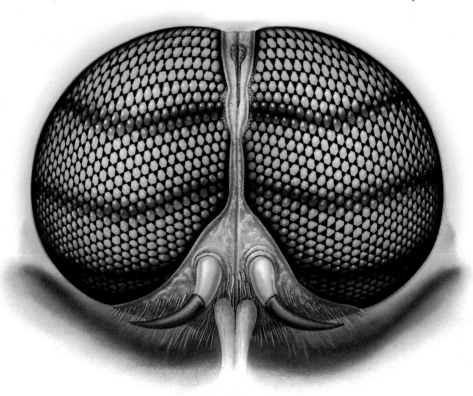

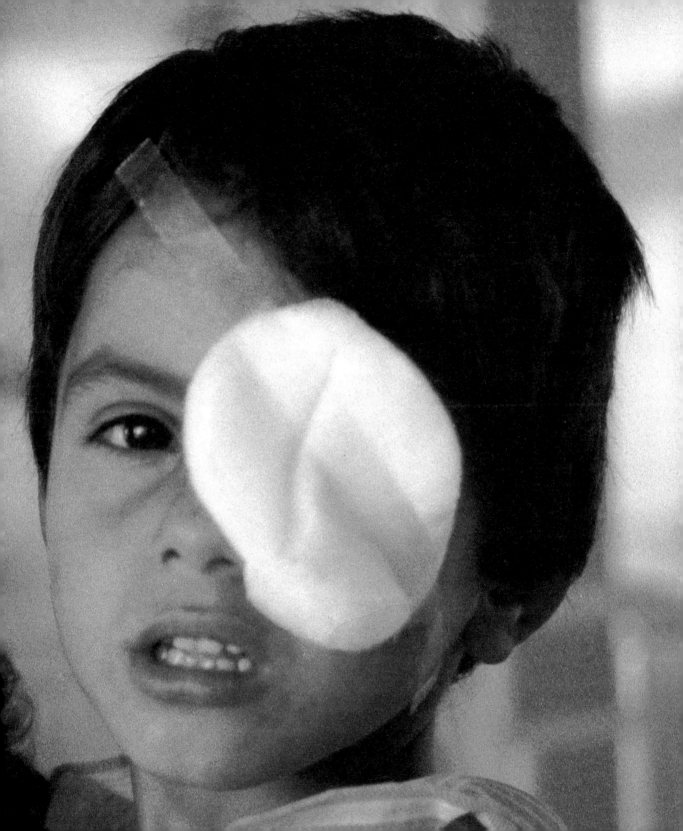

Looking around

We are able to move our eyes up and down and from side to side. This lets us read a page of a book without having to move our head. Sometimes we can spot something out of the corner of our eye. We can then turn our head to see it properly.

▷ We cannot see behind us without moving our head. But a frog has almost all round vision. This is because its eyes are positioned at the top of its head, not at the front, like ours.

▽ Three pairs of tiny muscles move our eyes in their sockets up, down and from side to side.

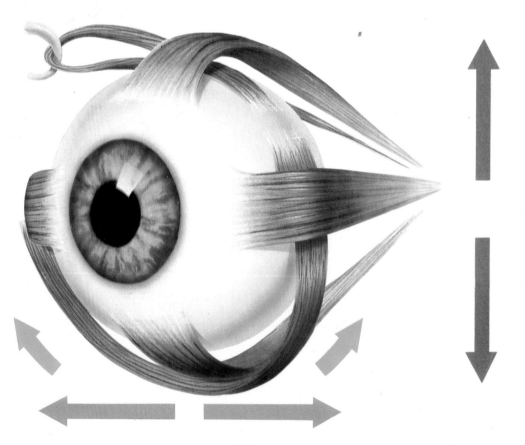

Can we believe our eyes?

As soon as we are born our eyes begin to see the world around us. We learn to recognise patterns and shapes. Our brains make sense of all the things we see around us. But sometimes our brains can be tricked by our eyes. We may see things that are not really there, or we may fail to see unusual or unexpected things!

▷ We learn to recognise the faces of other human beings at a very young age.

▽ Optical illusions trick our eyes into believing that something appears to be different from what it actually is.

◁ What can you see in this picture – a candlestick or two faces?

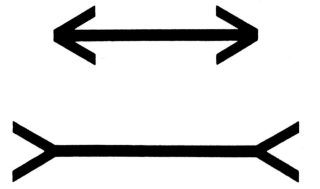

▽ Guess which line is longest. Then measure them both with a ruler.

Helping us see more

If we are lucky enough to have good eyesight, we may be able to see even more with help. Scientists have made some instruments that help us see very small things. A microscope lets us see tiny plants and animals. A telescope lets us see things that are very far away. We are able to see stars and planets that we cannot see with our eyes alone.

▷ The special lenses in a telescope make the moon look much closer.

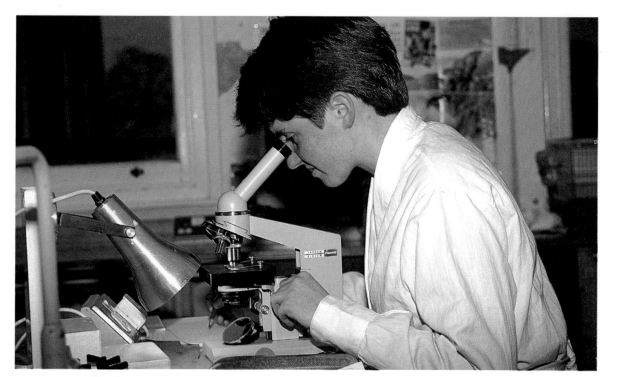

△ Microscopes magnify things, or make them look bigger, that are usually invisible to the naked eye, such as bacteria.

▷ We can use a hand lens, or magnifying glass, to help us see things close up.

Things to do

- Look in the mirror at the size of the pupil in the middle of your eye. Look at a bright light for a few seconds. Look at your pupils again. Then go into a dark room. Look at your pupils. What do you notice about their size?

- If you have a coat with a hood, check and see how far you can see around, first with the hood down and then with the hood up. Keep your head looking to the front for this test, and only move your eyes from side to side. What do you notice? If your hood cuts down the amount you can see, remember this when you are crossing a road and put your hood down.

- Use a drop of water on a piece of clear stiff plastic to make a lense to magnify the words in this book.

Glossary

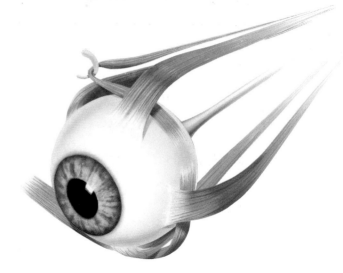

Braille A system of writing and printing for blind people, named after Louis Braille, the Frenchman who invented it whilst teaching the blind. In Braille, letters and numbers are represented by different arrangements of raised dots and are read by touching them.

colour blindness Not able to tell certain colours apart. Some colour blind people may see both red and green as the same shade of brown.

iris The coloured part of the eye around the pupil.

lens The part of the eye that focuses light rays on the retina. It is nearly round, and made up of layers of see-through cells, rather like an onion.

long-sighted Seeing distant things more clearly than near ones. Often people who are long-sighted need to wear glasses to read.

optic nerve The nerve that goes from rod and cone cells in the retina to the brain.

pupil The opening in the centre of the eye which looks like a black spot. The pupil is the only place where light can enter the eye. The iris can open or close the pupil so that the right amount of light falls on the retina.

retina The lining at the back of the eyeball that is sensitive to light and receives images of things looked at.

short-sighted Not able to see things far away clearly.

stereoscopic vision The ability to see things as solids, not flat.

Index

Photographic credits:
Chris Fairclough Colour Library
3, 15, 20, 29; Eye Ubiquitous
(J. Hazel)8; Eye Ubiquitous (Gavin
Wickham)13; Hutchison Library 23;
Peter Millard 11; Science Photo
Library 25; Spectrum Colour Library
4, 17, 27; John Walmsley Photo
Library 19; ZEFA Picture Library 7.